M.V.P.
Most Valuable Player

Earvin "Magic" Johnson

Bob Italia

Published by Abdo & Daughters, 6535 Cecilia Circle, Edina, Minnesota 55439.

Library bound edition distributed by Rockbottom Books, Pentagon Tower, P.O. Box 36036, Minneapolis, Minnesota 55435.

Printed in the United States.

Cover Photo: Allsport Photography USA, Inc.
Inside Photos: The Bettman Archive: 7, 14, 16, 19, 23, 25, 27, 31.
                Allsport Photography USA, Inc.: 4,

Edited by Rosemary Wallner

Library of Congress Cataloging-in-Publication Data

Italia, Robert, 1955-
        Magic Johnson / written by Bob Italia ; [edited by Rosemary Wallner].
        p. cm. -- (M.V.P. , most valuable player)

ISBN: 1-56239-120-8 (lib. bdg.)

1. Johnson, Earvin, 1959-   --Juvenile literature. 2. Basketball players--United States--Biography--Juvenile literature. 3. Los Angeles Lakers (Basketball team)--Juvenile litera-ture. I. Wallner, Rosemary, 1964-   . II. Title. III. Series: Italia, Robert, 1955-
M.V.P., most valuable player.
GV884.J63I83   1992
796.323'092--dc20
[B]
                                                    92-19754
                                                      CIP
                                                       AC

Contents

Earvin Johnson has been pure magic
on the basketball court.

The Man They Call "Magic"

There has never been a basketball player like him before, and there may never be one like him again. Standing 6 feet 9 inches, Earvin "Magic" Johnson handles the basketball better than most guards many inches shorter. His crisp passing and ability to run the court have made him a natural leader. Since he first stepped into a Los Angeles uniform in 1979, the Lakers have become one of the most successful basketball franchises in history.

Many sports fans credit Magic Johnson with turning the National Basketball Association (NBA) into the success story that it is today. His charming smile and youthful enthusiasm have become his trademark. And his pure athletic ability has made him a superstar.

Yet despite all his success, the Magic Johnson story is not without its tragic moments. No news event in recent memory was more distressful or shocking than the day Magic Johnson told the world he was retiring because he had acquired the AIDS virus.

Johnson's plight is tragic, but it also may prove to be invaluable to us all. Magic Johnson, a basketball champion all his life, has become the champion of a new and more important cause—the fight against the deadly AIDS disease. Through his brave and heroic efforts, the battle against AIDS may finally be won.

Playing Basketball in the Snow

Earvin Johnson, Jr., was born on August 14, 1959, in Lansing, Michigan. His father, Earvin, worked in the nearby Oldsmobile auto factory. Because he had such a large family and did not make much money, Johnson's father also worked two part-time jobs. Johnson's mother, Christine, stayed home and took care of Johnson and his five brothers and sisters.

Johnson came from a basketball family. Both his parents had played organized basketball when they were younger. During the basketball season, the Johnson's watched games on television whenever they could, and Johnson's father would always explain the game to his children. Once Johnson was big enough to dribble and shoot a basketball, he began playing the sport.

Johnson and his parents, Christine and Earvin.

Johnson's interest in basketball soon turned into a passion. He played whenever he could at a nearby playground. When winter came and covered the playground with snow, Johnson shoveled the basketball court so he could continue to develop his skills. His neighbors, watching Johnson jump around, thought he was crazy. They called him "June Bug Johnson."

When he entered Dwight Rich Junior High School, Johnson was six feet tall. Though he was skinny and not very strong, all his practicing on the playground was already paying off. The lanky Johnson had great coordination and balance. He dribbled the ball with ease, and his passing skills were outstanding. Even more, Johnson had an understanding of basketball strategies that most boys his age and older did not possess.

With these combined skills, Johnson was already a great basketball player. And because he was so good, he and his teammates enjoyed the game even more. That's why he always smiled and had a good time on the court.

On the Bus to Stardom

High school coaches from all around the Lansing area took notice of Johnson. One was George Fox of Everett High School. "We were all aware in junior high school that he'd be all-state some day," said Fox.

But Fox did not think he had much of a chance to get Johnson to play for his basketball team. The Lansing area was for the most part racially segregated. Everett High School was mostly white. Even more, it was farther away from Johnson's home than Sexton High School, which was mostly black. Fox and Johnson both knew that Johnson would eventually attend Sexton.

But then, when Johnson was in the ninth grade, something happened that broke down the racial barriers in Lansing's school system. The school board voted to bus both black and white students to different schools outside their neighborhoods. This decision gave black children a chance for a better education.

But Johnson didn't like the busing idea. "I was upset," he said. "I wanted to go to Sexton. I went to every Sexton game. I was a Sexton man, and then they came up with this busing thing." Despite his misgivings, Johnson signed up for classes at Everett.

Johnson was just like any other young man. It was hard for him to adjust to new surroundings. Despite the busing, Everett High School was still mostly white. And Johnson felt like an outsider. He had grown up in a black neighborhood and had attended black schools. All his friends were black as well.

There was one thing at Everett High School that made Johnson happy: basketball. Johnson quickly established himself as the star of the team. In nearly every game, he was the leading scorer and top rebounder and assist leader. He became the school hero—and made many new friends. Now, Everett High School wasn't such a bad place to be.

How Johnson Got His Nickname

Johnson's heroics on the basketball court soon brought him recognition outside his high school. Anyone who followed basketball in Michigan knew the name of Earvin Johnson. He often made headlines in the local newspapers, and sportswriters couldn't find the right words to describe Johnson's talent for basketball.

All but one sportswriter, that is. His name was Fred Stabley, Jr. Stabley wrote for *The Lansing State Journal.* In December 1974, Stabley, searching for those right words, suddenly came up with one of the most famous nicknames in all sports. He wrote that fifteen-year-old Earvin Johnson was "magic" on the court. "Magic" Johnson. The name seemed appropriate. And every time Stabley wrote about Johnson, he called him Magic Johnson. Soon everyone who followed Michigan basketball called Johnson "Magic."

Despite Johnson's talent, Everett High School never won a state championship during Johnson's first three years. Basketball is a team sport, and Johnson could not do it all. Still, Johnson was recognized as one of the top five high school basketball players in the country. Colleges from around the country offered Johnson basketball scholarships nearly every day. But Johnson had another year of high school. And most of all, he wanted to win a state championship.

In his senior year, Johnson led his team to a Number One ranking in Michigan. But they still had to win the state tournament before they could truly say they were Number One.

Johnson and his team made it to the championship game. There they encountered a tough team from Brother Rice High. The game went into overtime—and Johnson took control. Everett eventually won by six points, and people mobbed Johnson at the buzzer. For his efforts, Johnson was named "Prep Player of the Year" by United Press International (UPI), an international writing service. Not only was Johnson recognized as the top high school basketball player in Michigan, but in the entire country as well.

Magic Johnson Chooses a College

Now Magic Johnson had to concentrate on his college career. Yes, he wanted to play college basketball. But he also wanted to study communications in the hopes of someday becoming a sports announcer.

Johnson wanted to stay in Michigan. That left him with two choices: the University of Michigan in Ann Arbor, or Michigan State University in East Lansing. The University of Michigan had a very successful basketball program. Chances were good that Johnson would be playing for a nationally ranked team that received much attention from newspapers and television around the country.

Michigan State University did not have a very good basketball program. They were trying to build it into a good one, but were not there yet. The Spartans hadn't won a conference championship in twenty years. Despite the negative points about the university, Johnson's father wanted his son to attend Michigan State because it was close to home. And one of Johnson's friends, Jay Vincent, also would be attending Michigan State on a basketball scholarship.

Johnson liked the idea of going to a school where the team was struggling. He always considered himself an underdog, and thought that he could help Michigan State rebuild their basketball team. Finally, in April 1977, Magic Johnson announced that he would be attending Michigan State University.

Johnson arrived as a celebrity on the Michigan State campus that fall. He was a very likable, carefree, and friendly person who liked to attend parties and go on dates with the new girls he met. But he was very serious when it came to basketball. With Johnson, Vincent, and junior Gregory Kelser, Michigan State had a solid team on which to build their program. By February 1978, Michigan State had already won twenty games—more than they had won in seventy-nine seasons!

Johnson, who played point guard, finished his first season with impressive statistics. He was first in the Big Ten conference in assists, tied for third in scoring, and sixth in rebounding. For his efforts, Johnson was named a college All-American—the only freshman in the nation to receive such an honor.

Johnson and the Spartans reached the NCAA tournament that same year. But Johnson and Vincent were still young and inexperienced, and did not do well against the better teams in the country. Western Kentucky eliminated the Spartans from the tournament in the semifinals.

Despite the loss, professional basketball scouts were impressed with Johnson. They tempted him with huge salary offers to skip his remaining college years and turn pro. The young Johnson listened very hard. "It wasn't so much the fact of all that money as it was finally realizing the dream of being a professional that I've had so long," he said.

Johnson's mother was against the idea. She wanted Johnson to get his college degree. Johnson's father was against the idea as well. He thought his son was too young, and wanted Johnson to wait until he was ready to turn pro. Johnson reluctantly agreed.

Magic and the Bird

The following season, Johnson played forward. The Spartans finished with a 21-6 record and again made it to the NCAA tournament semifinals. This time, Johnson was ready for the competition, and the Spartans easily won their contest over the University of Pennsylvania. Now they were in the finals against Indiana State University and their star player, Larry Bird. The winner would be crowned national champion.

Magic Johnson and Larry Bird talk to the press
before their NCAA showdown.

Larry Bird was a bigger star than Magic Johnson. He had a higher scoring average, and he played for a team that was 32-0. But Johnson and the Spartans played tough against Bird, limiting him to only 19 points. Meanwhile, Johnson scored 24 points and had many assists to his teammates. The Spartans' balanced attack was too much for Bird and Indiana State to overcome, and the Spartans won the national championship 75-64.

Now, the demand for Magic Johnson's basketball talents was even greater. The pressure to turn pro was incredible—especially since it guaranteed that Johnson would become a rich young man. Johnson promised his mother that he would get his degree by attending summer school. She seemed happy with the promise. As for Johnson's father, he had no doubt that his son was now ready for professional sports. So Magic Johnson declared himself eligible for the 1979 draft and waited for a team to pick him in the first round.

He didn't have to wait long. The Los Angeles Lakers had the very first pick, and they chose Earvin Magic Johnson. The Lakers offered Johnson $600,000 a year for four years, which Johnson accepted. It was good money for a nineteen-year-old.

*Johnson was all smiles after the Los Angeles Lakers
made him their Number One pick in the NBA draft.*

A Magic Season

The Lakers expected big things from Johnson right away, and that put much pressure on him. Johnson would play point guard and be responsible for most of the ball-handling. But he was also expected to score—and often.

In Johnson's first game, October 12, 1979, against the San Diego Clippers, his inexperience showed. Johnson was not used to the physical game that professionals played, and he only scored one point in the first seventeen minutes. Coach Jack McKinney benched Johnson for a while, then put Magic back into the game. Johnson responded by finishing with 26 points as the Lakers won 103-102.

Throughout the season, Johnson proved he was worthy of being the Number One pick in the draft. He thrilled crowds everywhere with his ball handling and play-making. He seemed to know where everyone was on the court and where they were going—even before they did! Johnson quickly became famous for his no-look passes, where he would look one way and pass the other—often for a teammate's easy basket.

But most of all, Johnson became famous for his easy-going style and ear-to-ear grin. He made basketball enjoyable for the players and the fans everywhere.

Though he did not receive rookie-of-the-year honors (that award went to Larry Bird of the Boston Celtics), Johnson helped the Lakers reach the NBA championship series against the Philadelphia 76ers. It was a hard-fought series that the Lakers led 3-2 as they went to Philadelphia for Game 6.

The Lakers' star player, center Kareem Abdul-Jabbar, did not make the trip to Philadelphia. He had hurt his ankle in Game 5 and could not play. That's when the Lakers made a strange move. They decided to start rookie Magic Johnson at center for Game 6.

Basketball fans around the country thought the Lakers were crazy. But Johnson had always been a great rebounder, and was up for the challenge. Johnson played tough against Philadelphia center Darryl Dawkins. He kept Dawkins at bay and brought down rebound after rebound.

Then late in the fourth quarter, with the Lakers clinging to a 1-point lead, Magic Johnson led his teammates on a scoring spree. When the final buzzer sounded, the scoreboard showed 123-107 in favor of the Lakers. Amazingly, the 6-9, 220-pound Johnson had scored 42 points and had pulled down 15 rebounds. For his efforts, Johnson was named Most Valuable Player of the championship series.

*Johnson was named the MVP of the
1980 NBA Championship series.*

Johnson's incredible performance amazed people all across the nation. Here he was, a rookie point guard, and he had just led his team to a championship as a center! It was a feat never seen before in professional basketball— and vaulted Magic Johnson into the national spotlight reserved for superstars.

Twenty-year-old Earvin Magic Johnson was on top of the world—and never happier. The press and fans mobbed Johnson everywhere he went. He signed endorsement contracts with 7-Up, Converse athletic shoes, and Spalding basketballs. And when he went home that summer to attend school, the townspeople greeted him as a hero. It was truly a magic season for Earvin Johnson.

It Only Gets Better

The 1980-81 season was a disappointment for Magic Johnson. He suffered a knee injury that required surgery, and he missed forty-five games. It was the first time Johnson had been seriously injured, and at first he did not know how to handle it. But Johnson learned a valuable lesson. "It made me see that everything came fast and good and that it could easily be taken away just as fast," he said.

The Lakers made the playoffs that year, but eventually lost to the Houston Rockets. Despite the disappointing season, the Lakers signed Johnson to one of the biggest sports contracts ever—one million dollars a year for twenty-five years!

There was much resentment among his teammates over the huge contract. But Johnson shrugged off the criticism and played his best the next season, leading the Lakers to another NBA championship.

Johnson and the Lakers found themselves in the playoffs again in the 1982-83 season, but they lost to the Philadelphia 76ers in the finals. The Lakers regrouped the following season and returned to their championship form, winning the Western Conference for the fourth time in five years. Now Johnson would get to face his old basketball nemesis—Larry Bird of the Boston Celtics.

Johnson played one of his most memorable championship series ever. He set a record for most playoff assists (25) and averaged 18 points a game. But Johnson also set a record for the most turnovers, and Boston won the NBA championship. For one of the few times in his life, Johnson came to know the bitter taste of failure.

It was a long summer before the 1984-85 season began. But it remained a magical time for Johnson. He bought a new five-bedroom house in the exclusive Bel Air neighborhood near Los Angeles, California. He spent much time decorating the home just right, sparing no expense.

It was a big home for the young bachelor. And although he was dating Cookie Kelly, a department store manager he had met in Toledo, Ohio, seven year earlier, Johnson was in no hurry to get married.

Johnson dated other women as well. There didn't seem any reason to get married. He was young and rich and handsome, and he could have anything he wanted.

The next season turned out much better for Johnson and the Lakers. They made it to the NBA finals again and earned a rematch with the Boston Celtics. This time, Magic Johnson was ready to lead his team to victory. He played his usual brilliant game and eliminated the costly turnovers. When the hard-fought series ended, Johnson and the Lakers stood victorious. Finally, Johnson had beaten Larry Bird in an important professional game. There seemed little left to do in his storybook life.

The 1985 championship seemed to mature Magic Johnson. He became engaged to Cookie Kelly and started making plans to return to a simple life once he retired from basket- ball. But in the 1986 playoffs, the Dallas Mavericks stunned the Lakers. For the first time in four years, the Lakers didn't make the NBA finals. Now Johnson had a new ax to grind. He vowed to help the Lakers return to the finals, and com- mitted himself to basketball like he had never done before.

This new committment left little time for his personal life. Johnson decided to call off his engagement to Cookie Kelly. "I can't get married now," he said. "Not while I'm still married to basketball." When Johnson would give up his basketball career was anyone's guess. He was still on top of his game, and there was always another season to show the world he was one of the best basketball players ever.

The 1986-87 season proved to be one of the best for Johnson and the Lakers. Johnson averaged a career-high 23.9 points per game and led the league in assists with a 12.2 average. And the Lakers finished with a remarkable 65-17 record—one of the best ever. To top it all off, the league named Johnson its Most Valuable Player—only the third guard in NBA history to win the award.

The Lakers cruised through the playoffs and met the Boston Celtics in the finals. Johnson made the game-winning shot in Game 4 in Boston, then the Lakers wrapped up the championship in Game 6. Johnson was the MVP of the series. It was truly Magic Johnson's greatest season ever.

Johnson received the MVP award for the
1987 Championship series.

The following year, 1988, the Lakers won the championship again—making them the first team in nineteen years to win back-to-back titles. Now Johnson had another goal in mind—to lead his team to a third consecutive championship.

But standing in the way were Isiah Thomas and the Detroit Pistons who had established themselves as the new power in the NBA. The Lakers and Pistons eventually met in the 1989 championship series, but the Pistons prevailed. Still, the NBA voted Johnson as MVP for the second time. The next season, Johnson won his first All-Star MVP award as he led the Lakers to a 63-19 finish. Though the Lakers were eliminated in the playoffs, Magic Johnson became the sixth player in NBA history to win consecutive MVP awards—his third in four years.

Johnson's last appearance in the NBA finals came in 1991 against Michael Jordan and the Chicago Bulls. It was a dream match-up between two of the most talented basketball players ever—Magic and Jordan. Though Jordan and the Bulls got the best of the Lakers, Magic Johnson played his usual brilliant game. He looked forward to the following year with all the enthusiasm of a rookie. Johnson was already hoping and plotting for a rematch against the Bulls.

*Johnson battled Michael Jordan
in the 1991 Championship series.*

Magic Johnson had had a remarkable career. There were few milestones left for him to reach. Johnson had done it all and won it all. Now it was time for him to accomplish some personal goals. Johnson became engaged to Cookie Kelly again. And this time he honored his committment to her. On September 14, 1991, Johnson married Kelly. Though Johnson wanted to play basketball, he was—finally—looking to the future.

The Day the Dream Life Died

Magic Johnson had led a storybook life. He was rich, famous, and successful. Everything he did turned to gold, and he could do no wrong. He seemed superhuman, invulnerable to anything that was bad. Young people everywhere wanted to be like Magic Johnson.

But then on November 7, 1991, Magic Johnson's storybook life suddenly turned into a nightmare.

It all started when the 32-year-old superstar spoke these fateful words at a televised press conference: "Because of the HIV virus I have obtained, I will have to announce my retirement from the Lakers today."

With his wife Cookie at his side, Johnson announced to the world that he had tested positive for the HIV virus.

Days earlier, Johnson had missed the Lakers' final exhibition game and first three regular season games because of fatigue and flu-like symptoms. But as it turned out, his illness was much more serious than first suspected.

On October 25, 1991, test results from a physical exam came back with very bad news: there was the possibility that the AIDS virus was present in Magic Johnson's blood stream. Johnson needed more tests. Then there was no doubt. Magic Johnson had tested positive for the human immunodeficiency virus (HIV).

Just like that, the storybook life was over. The NBA suddenly lost one of its brightest stars. The world had lost one of its most admired and talented athletes. For Magic Johnson had now entered a deadly battle against AIDS (Acquired Immune Deficiency Syndrome). It is the HIV virus that eventually causes AIDS—and so far, there is no cure.

Johnson was charming, pleasant, and courageous at the press conference, still wearing the broad white smile that always accompanies him. He refused to admit defeat, promising to become a spokesperson against AIDS while personally battling the disease. He admitted having been naive about AIDS, then sent a chilling message to all: "Here I am saying it can happen to anybody, even me, Magic Johnson." Then he reassured the nation that his wife, two months pregnant, had tested negative for the virus.

Johnson was forced to retire because he needed to save his strength to fight the HIV virus. The strenuous playing schedule maintained by the Lakers would only wear Johnson down.

Though Johnson has the HIV virus, he does not have AIDS. None of the AIDS symptoms have shown yet. But it is only a matter of time. How much time is anyone's guess. It could be ten years or more before Johnson begins suffering from the disease.

The shock of the tragic news traveled around the world, and rekindled the fears and concerns about AIDS. Children in schools and on playgrounds hung their heads in sadness. Every basketball game in every NBA arena held a moment of prayer or silence for Magic Johnson as players openly wept for their friend.

But Johnson decided to fight that tragic view. The very next night, he was on "The Arsenio Hall Show" explaining his views and preaching his message about AIDS. Yes, he had the HIV virus. But he was still alive and healthy. And he planned on being around for a long, long time while battling the disease.

Later, Johnson admitted he was careless. He did not use a condom when having sex with a woman who had the HIV virus—that's how he contracted the virus. (Having unprotected sex with someone is just one way a person can aquire AIDS. To find out more about AIDS, you can call the National AIDS Hotline at 1-800-342-AIDS.)

There are those who say that Magic Johnson's promiscuity has led him to his downfall, and that he does not deserve the status of American hero and role model. Perhaps. But instead of hiding his ailment or denying its existence, he stood before the nation and bravely broke the news. For that act alone, he should be commended.

Despite all the bad news surrounding Johnson, there remains this positive point: Magic Johnson is perhaps the perfect candidate to carry the message of AIDS awareness to people everywhere. He knows this, and has bravely accepted the challenge. In that respect, Magic Johnson is a true American hero.

Life Goes On

Though the future looks very dark for Magic Johnson, there is always the hope that a cure for AIDS will be developed before the symptoms appear in him. Until that day arrives, Magic Johnson will devote his precious time educating people about the HIV virus and AIDs.

Basketball will still be a big part of Magic Johnson's life. He has accepted an invitation to play on the 1992 U.S. Olympic Basketball Team. It is a "dream" team composed of the N.B.A.'s finest players.

Johnson also hopes that one day he will own a professional basketball franchise, but that remains to be seen. (Some estimates place Johnson's worth at $100 million. Besides his endorsements for companies like Pepsi and Kentucky Fried Chicken, Johnson owns a T-shirt company and a Pepsi distributorship).

"I'm not fearing it," said Magic Johnson of his battle against AIDS. "I'm not down. I'm here saying I got it. I plan on going on living for a long time. You don't have to run from me. You can give me my hugs, my high fives, my kisses.

Johnson's legacy as an MVP will always be remembered.

If I die tomorrow, I've had the greatest life anybody could ever imagine."

Win or lose, Earvin "Magic" Johnson has always been a courageous fighter—someone we can all admire. He has already left us a basketball legacy that will be talked about for years to come—and glorious memories that will last forever.

Magic's Legacy

- NBA Most Valuable Player—1987, 1989, 1990
- Member of the All-NBA First Team—1983-91
- Playoff MVP—1980, 1982, 1987
- All-Star Game MVP—1990
- Member of NBA Championship Team—1980, 1982, 1985, 1987-88
- All-time assist leader—9,921
- Member of NCAA championship team—1979

Magic Johnson's Address

If you would like to write to Magic Johnson, or join the fight against AIDS, send your letters to:

Magic Johnson Foundation
1801 Avenue of the Stars
Suite 344
Los Angeles, CA 90067